THE VIETNAM WAR

Complete and Engaging Account of
Vietnam War (Southeast Asia)

By

Charles William

NOTE

The Vietnam War, spanning from 1955 to 1975, was a brutal conflict rooted in the desire to unify Vietnam under communist ideology. On one side stood the communist forces of North Vietnam, led by the Democratic Republic of Vietnam and supported by the Viet Cong, indigenous fighters in the south. Opposing them were the anti-communist Republic of Vietnam, also known as South Vietnam, and its allies, primarily the United States.

Ho Chi Minh, the leader of North Vietnam, sought to reunify the country after decades of colonization and foreign influence. The war escalated with the involvement of major powers, including the Soviet Union and China backing the communist North, and the United States leading the anti-communist effort in the South.

The conflict saw significant deployment of U.S. military personnel, starting with advisers in the 1950s and escalating to combat troops by the mid-1960s. The war was marked by fierce battles, devastating casualties, and widespread destruction.

Ultimately, on April 30, 1975, the war concluded with the fall of Saigon, the capital of South Vietnam, to North Vietnamese forces. This marked the end of a long and painful chapter in Vietnam's history, but its impact would resonate for generations to come.

Table of Contents

INTRODUCTION	**8**
CHAPTER 1	**13**
HISTORY TO 1949	**13**
CHAPTER 2	**19**
EXIT OF THE FRENCH, 1950-1955	**19**
CHAPTER 3	**22**
THE DIEM ERA, 1955-1963	**22**
COUP AND ASSASSINATIONS	26
CHAPTER 4	**30**
ESCALATION AND AMERICANIZATION, 1963-1968	**30**
GULF OF TONKIN AND THE WESTMORELAND EXPANSION	30
OPERATION ROLLING THUNDER, 1965-1968	34
THE BIG BUILD-UP	36
SEARCH AND DESTROY	39
THE HO CHI MINH TRAIL	41
THE TET OFFENSIVE	43
PARIS PEACE TALKS	45
CHAPTER 5	**49**

VIETNAMIZATION AND AMERICAN WITHDRAWAL, 1969-1974	**49**
RICHARD NIXON'S PURSUIT OF PEACE WITH HONOR	49
OPERATION MENU AND THE CAMBODIAN INCURSION, 1969-1970	51
THE EASTER OFFENSIVE	54
U.S. PRESIDENTIAL ELECTION OF 1972 AND OPERATION LINEBACKER II	56
RETURN TO PARIS	57
CHAPTER 6	**61**
SOUTH VIETNAM STANDS ALONE, 1974 – 1975	**61**
TOTAL U.S. WITHDRAWAL	61
CAMPAIGN 275	64
FINAL NORTH VIETNAMESE OFFENSIVE	67
FALL OF SAIGON	70
CHAPTER 7	**73**
AFTERMATH	**73**
CHAPTER 8	**77**
OTHER COUNTRIES' INVOLVEMENT	**77**
THE SOVIET UNION	77
PEOPLE'S REPUBLIC OF CHINA	78
REPUBLIC OF KOREA	80
DEMOCRATIC PEOPLE'S REPUBLIC OF KOREA	82
AUSTRALIA AND NEW ZEALAND	83
THAILAND	85
CANADA	87
CHAPTER 9	**89**

USE OF CHEMICAL DEFOLIANTS 89

CONCLUSION 94

LEGAL NOTICE

This book, or any portion of it, may not be reprinted in any kind deposited in a retrieval system or distributed in any format by any method, be it electronic, mechanical, photocopied, recorded, or otherwise in any form without the publisher's written permission, except as permitted copyright law of the United States of America.

DISCLAIMER

All materials in this book are for educational and informational purposes only. Can accept no responsibility for any effects or results obtained from the use of this material.

Although every effort has been made to provide correct and adequate information, the author assumes no responsibility for the accuracy, use, or misuse of such information.

Copyright © 2024 by Charles William

All Rights Reserved

Introduction

An ideological war in Vietnam's deep jungles and busy cities sparked flames that spread across nations and influenced history. Welcome to the fierce saga of the Vietnam War—a captivating tale of power, passion, and the relentless pursuit of a unified nation.

It began with a fervent vision in the heart of Ho Chi Minh, who yearned to knit together the fabric of Vietnam into a single, communist state. For Ho, the scars of colonization ran deep, echoing the struggles against French rule in the First Indochina War. With the Democratic Republic of Vietnam and the indomitable Việt Cộng by his side, Ho Chi Minh stood against the Republic of Vietnam and its staunch allies, led prominently by the United States.

The world watched with fear as the Cold War cast its ominous shadow over the conflict, turning Vietnam into a battleground of ideologies. From the towering skyscrapers of New York to the ancient alleyways of Hanoi, the echoes of war thundered, drawing nations into a deadly move of power and politics.

The United States, with its military might and unwavering resolve, poured troops and resources into the fray, entangling itself deeply in the quagmire of Southeast Asia. From the first whispers of military advisers in 1950 to the thunderous roar of combat troops in 1965, America's involvement escalated, leaving an unforgettable mark on history.

Yet, amid the chaos and carnage, the true cost of war lay in its human toll. Over 2.5 million lives, from Vietnamese villages to Cambodian towns, were claimed by the relentless tide of conflict. Civilians bore the brunt of the suffering, their lives shattered by the clash of empires and the struggle for supremacy.

Finally, on that fateful month of April 1975, the war reached its climax as the streets of Saigon fell silent under the triumphant footsteps of North Vietnamese forces. The world watched the horror as the curtain closed on one of the most divisive chapters of modern history.

But the scars of Vietnam didn't fade so easily. Across the oceans, in the corridors of power and the hearts of the people, the war stirred a tempest of controversy and dissent. The American nation was generally successful in its military activities in Vietnam, but it failed to acquire public support from the States, and the war prompted a significant deal of opposition in the United States making President Lyndon B. Johnson decide not to run for reelection in 1968 due to his poor handling of the war.

In the wake of the rough late 1960s, the promise of a new dawn beckoned with the election of Richard Nixon to the presidency in 1968. With whispers of a "secret plan" for a dignified withdrawal from Vietnam, Nixon captured the hopes of a war-weary nation. Yet, his vision for ending the conflict takes shape in both bold and controversial ways.

Steering away from his predecessor's strategy of direct engagement, Nixon unveiled his masterstroke: "Vietnamization." This audacious plan sought to shift the burden of combat onto the shoulders of Vietnamese troops while focusing American efforts on pacification and development.

Under this banner, education and progress pave the path to peace in the embattled lands of South Vietnam.

In the account of history, Nixon's gambit bore fruit. Just in 1969 alone, thousands of pro-communist forces laid down their arms, signaling a turning tide in the war's narrative. However, amidst this ray of progress, Nixon's resolve faces its greatest test.

In a move that resonated across the globe, Nixon dared to breach the borders of conventional warfare, venturing into Cambodia in 1970 to root out North Vietnamese sanctuaries. The decision ignited a fierce debate, yet Nixon remained resolute in his pursuit of peace through strength.

As the 1972 presidential elections loomed large, the specter of war cast a shadow over the political landscape. When North Vietnam abruptly withdrew from peace talks, Nixon's response was swift and decisive—a relentless bombing campaign that compelled the enemy back to the negotiating table in Paris.

But even as Nixon's foreign policy victories painted a picture of triumph, storm clouds gathered on the home front. The Watergate scandal, a dark stain on the fabric of American democracy, eroded Nixon's once-unassailable support. In the halls of Congress, opposition grew, culminating in a decisive cutoff of aid to South Vietnam.

In August 1974, as the walls of scandal closed in, Nixon made the ultimate sacrifice for the nation he once led, resigning from office in disgrace. Yet, the fallout of his downfall echoes far beyond the borders of Washington.

In the lonely aftermath of Vietnam's fall to communism, a groundbreaking shift reshaped the geopolitical landscape. From Southeast Asia to Africa and beyond, the Soviet sphere of influence expanded, marking the end of America's hegemonic reign as the "world's policeman."

While the dust settled on the battlefields of Vietnam, one undeniable truth emerged: victory or defeat was not etched in the sands of war, but written in the hearts and minds of the American people. The Vietnam War became a cautionary tale—a reminder that in the trial of conflict, the court of public opinion reigns supreme, shaping the destiny of nations for generations to come.

Chapter 1

History to 1949

From the depths of antiquity to the brink of modernity, Vietnam's narrative unfolds against the backdrop of shifting empires and steadfast resistance. For centuries, the land we now know as Vietnam lay trapped within the embrace of China, save for fleeting moments of independence.

Emerging from the shadows of foreign dominion, Vietnam embarked on a journey marked by rebellion and resilience. Yet, as one oppressor decreased, another emerged, casting its shadow over the land. In the throes of the 19th century, the specter of French colonialism threatened large, as

Indochina became a battleground in a series of colonial wars.

As the world rocked on the brink of war, Vietnam's struggle for independence found a voice on the global stage. At the post-World War I negotiations in 1919, Ho Chí Minh, a visionary leader with a fervent desire for liberation, sought to carve out a path to freedom for the Indochinese colonies. Yet, his pleas fell on deaf ears, as the colonial powers stuck to their dominion over the region.

Amidst the chaos of the Second World War, Vietnam found itself caught in the crossfire of imperial ambitions. With the government of Vichy France capitulating to Japanese forces, the specter of Japanese occupation loomed large over Indochina. However, in the unrest, seeds of resistance were sown, as Ho Chí Minh rallied his compatriots to defy the oppressors.

In the trial of World War II, alliances shifted and loyalties were tested. With confidential support from the U.S. Office of Strategic Services, Ho Chí Minh marshaled his forces to oppose the occupiers, laying the groundwork for a new chapter in Vietnam's struggle for liberation.

In a dramatic turn of events, the Japanese overthrew the French administration in 1944, granting Vietnam nominal independence. While the dust settled on the battlefield, Vietnam stood on the cusp of a new dawn.

On September 2, 1945, amidst the jubilant cries of a nation yearning for freedom, Ho Chí Minh proclaimed the birth of a new era. Inspired by the ideals of liberty and independence, he invoked the spirit of America's Declaration of Independence, dreaming of a future where Vietnam stood as a sovereign nation.

Yet, on the euphoria of independence, uncertainty lingered on the horizon. Would the promises of liberation be realized, or would new challenges emerge to test the resolve of Vietnam's brave sons and daughters? Only time would tell, as the wheels of destiny continued to turn, shaping the fate of a nation and its people.

After World War II, the fate of Vietnam dangled, caught between the shifting tides of global politics and the phantom of colonial ambition. As the embers of war fumed, Ho Chí Minh, a beacon of hope for Vietnamese independence, stood at the forefront of a nation yearning to break free from the shackles of foreign rule.

In February 1946, amidst the echoes of a world in turmoil, Ho Chí Minh penned a desperate plea to President Harry S. Truman, beseeching American aid to stave off the impending threat of French domination. Yet, even as his words crossed oceans, events unfolded that would forever alter the course of Vietnam's destiny.

At the Potsdam Conference, the Allies, in a fateful decree, enacted that Vietnam would fall under the joint occupation of Nationalist Chinese and British forces. With the stroke of a pen, Vietnam's fate was sealed, as foreign armies descended upon its shores to supervise the surrender of the vanquished Japanese.

In the north, the Chinese army swept down from the mountains, their presence casting a shadow over Ho's fledgling government. Meanwhile, in the south, the British arrived, overseeing the departure of Japanese forces and paving the way for French resurgence.

As French officials emerged from the ashes of Japanese prisons, they wasted no time in reclaiming their lost dominion. In the north, negotiations staggered on the edge of a knife, as Ho Chí Minh made a delicate move with his former colonial masters.

In a daring plot, the French conceded Shanghai and other concessions in China to secure their foothold in northern Vietnam. Ho, seizing the opportunity, welcomed French forces with cautious optimism, envisioning a future where Vietnam stood as a beacon of independence within the French Union.

Nevertheless, as negotiations faltered and promises turned to ash, the drums of war thundered once more. In a brutal display of force, French bombardments rained down on Haiphong, leaving an imprint of destruction in their wake. Ho and the Việt Minh, their dreams of independence shattered, retreated into the rugged mountains, heralding the dawn of a new conflict—the First Indochina War.

But amidst the chaos, a flash of hope emerged on the horizon. With the triumph of the Communists in the Chinese Civil War, Premier Mao Zedong extended a hand of solidarity to the Viet Minh, offering military assistance and expertise. Armed with modern weapons and unwavering resolve, the Viet Minh stood ready to defy the forces of colonial oppression and forge their own path to freedom.

While the stage was set for a new chapter in Vietnam's rough history, the echoes of war rolled across the land, proof of the indomitable spirit of a people determined to carve out their destiny in the uproar of the times.

Chapter 2

Exit of the French, 1950-1955

As the flames of conflict engulfed the verdant landscapes of Indochina, a new player emerged on the stage of history, reshaping the course of the Vietnam War and laying the groundwork for a new era of turmoil and transformation.

In the corridors of power in Washington, the United States watched with growing concern as the specter of communism cast its shadow over the jungles of Vietnam. What had once been perceived as a colonial war now threatened large as a battleground in the global struggle against communism, orchestrated by the Kremlin.

In 1950, as the Korean War erupted in a blaze of violence, the United States pivoted its gaze towards Vietnam, viewing it through the lens of Cold War geopolitics. With a sense of urgency, the U.S. Military Assistance and Advisory Group (MAAG) descended upon the war-torn land, screening French requests for aid, advising on strategy, and training Vietnamese soldiers.

Armed with a staggering array of weaponry and a war chest packed with resources, the United States threw its weight behind the faltering French colonial effort. By 1954, over 300,000 small arms and machine guns, along with a staggering one billion dollars, had poured into Vietnam, shouldering the lion's share of the French military burden.

Yet, even as the drums of war echoed across the land, fate delivered a decisive blow to the colonial ambitions of France. On the hallowed grounds of Điện Biên Phủ, the Viet Minh unleashed a torrent of fury, inflicting a crushing defeat upon their erstwhile oppressors.

In the wake of this stunning victory, the tide of public opinion turned against the French, hastening their retreat from the blood-soaked fields of Vietnam. At the Geneva Conference, the French government bowed to the inevitable, negotiating a peace agreement with the Viet Minh that paved the way for their exit from Indochina.

However, even in victory, the specter of a division dominated Vietnam's future. Temporarily partitioned at the 17th parallel, the nation stood on the brink of a new chapter in its rugged history. Above the line, the Viet Minh established a socialist state—the Democratic Republic of Vietnam—while below, a non-communist regime took root under the supervision of Emperor Bảo Đại.

But the winds of change blew swiftly across the land, as Ngo Dinh Diem, Prime Minister under Bảo Đại, seized the reins of power, ousting the emperor and establishing himself as President of the young Republic of Vietnam.

Chapter 3

The Diem Era, 1955-1963

In the wake of the Geneva Accords of 1954, Vietnam stood at a crossroads, teetering on the precipice of uncertainty and change. As the specter of division loomed large over the nation, the promise of reunification hung in the balance, awaiting the outcome of free elections for a national leadership.

However, as the appointed hour for national reconciliation approached, the Diem government emerged as a staunch opponent of the Geneva Accords, refusing to entertain the prospect of reunification through elections. Encouraged by the unwavering support of the United States, Diem's regime stood firm against the tide of communist influence, determined to chart its own course within the swirling currents of Cold War politics.

At the heart of the Diem regime lay a figure both enigmatic and divisive. A devout Roman Catholic, Diem ruled with an iron fist, his aloof demeanor and closed-mindedness alienating allies and adversaries alike. Yet, in the eyes of the United States, he stood as a defense against the encroaching tide of communism, a natural ally in the fight for freedom and democracy.

In a series of bold maneuvers, Diem swept aside political opposition, launching military operations against dissenting factions with ruthless efficiency. From the Cao Dai Sect to the Hoa Hao and the Binh Xuyen organized crime group, no challenge to his authority went unanswered, cementing his grip on power with an iron fist.

Amidst the turmoil of repression, Diem orchestrated a facade of democracy, organizing elections for president and legislature while crafting a new constitution. Yet, as the ballots were cast and the votes tallied, accusations of electoral fraud echoed across the land, tarnishing the legitimacy of Diem's rule.

In a landslide victory that defied belief, Diem emerged triumphant, securing a staggering 98.2 percent of the vote—a victory marred by allegations of manipulation and coercion.

In the sweltering heat of the summer of 1955, a new chapter unfolded in the records of South Vietnam's history, as Ngo Dinh Diem, emboldened by his grip on power, launched a crusade against opponents of the state. With ruthless determination, Diem embarked on a campaign to root out perceived enemies of the state, launching a chilling "Denounce the Communists" crusade. Across South Vietnam, dissenters and anti-government elements found themselves ensnared in the web of Diem's iron grip, facing arrest, imprisonment, or even execution.

While the crackdown intensified, a tide of refugees and regroupees surged across the boundary line, seeking sanctuary from the encroaching specter of tyranny. In a staggering exodus, over 52,000 civilians fled southward, while a staggering 450,000 were airlifted or ferried across the divide, their hopes and dreams torn asunder by the winds of political upheaval.

Yet, even as Diem tightened his grip on power, the seeds of dissent took root, blossoming into a low-level insurgency that engulfed the nation in flames. In the shadows of South Vietnam, Viet Minh cadres, encouraged by their confidential caches of weaponry, began to wage a secret war against the regime.

In the corridors of power in Hanoi, whispers of reunification echoed through the hallowed halls, as Lê Duẩn urged the Vietnam Workers' Party to take a firmer stance against the forces of division. But hesitation lingered, casting a pall over the prospect of full-scale military confrontation.

Nonetheless, as the tide of history inexorably turned, the die was cast. In a daring gambit, on December 12, 1960, under the watchful gaze of Hanoi, southern communists forged a formidable alliance—the National Front for the Liberation of South Vietnam. A motley coalition of intellectuals, nationalists, and hardened revolutionaries, the NLF emerged as a potent force, poised to challenge the dominance of Diem's regime.

The conflict escalated, and the lines between ideology and nationalism blurred, with the NLF presenting itself as a broad-based movement for liberation, rather than a mere pawn of communist ambition.

Coup and Assassinations

Some persons in the corridors of power in Washington begin the whispers of doubt in the swirled-like smoke, casting a shadow over South Vietnam and the embattled reign of President Diem. As the shade of communism loomed ever on the horizon, some policymakers began to question Diem's ability to stem the tide of insurgency, fearing that he might even entertain the notion of a pact with the enemy.

Amidst the heat of the summer of 1963, discussions unfolded within the hallowed halls of the Kennedy administration, grappling with the possibility of regime change in Saigon. While the State Department championed the idea and encouraged a coup, the Pentagon and CIA remained wary, cognizant of the potential for destabilization in the wake of such an intense shift.

At the heart of the proposed changes lay the figure of Ngo Dinh Nhu, Diem's younger brother and the architect of South Vietnam's secret police apparatus. Feared and reviled by many, Nhu stood accused of orchestrating a campaign of repression against Buddhist dissidents, staining the regime's reputation both at home and abroad.

As pressure mounted and consensus coalesced, the decision was made to withdraw U.S. support from the Diem regime—a move endorsed by President Kennedy himself.

In November, a sinister plot unfolded on the streets of Saigon—a conspiracy born of treachery and ambition, with echoes that would resound across the rugged landscape of South Vietnam.

At the command of the U.S. embassy, whispers of discord found fertile ground among the ranks of military officers, fueling a coup d'état that would shake the very foundations of power. In a swift and merciless stroke, President Diem was toppled from his perch of authority, his fate sealed by the cold

28

hand of betrayal. Alongside his brother, he met a fierce end, their lives snuffed out in the crucible of political upheaval.

As the dust settled on the blood-stained streets of Saigon, chaos reigned supreme, casting a gloom of uncertainty over the fate of South Vietnam. Within the corridors of power in Hanoi, opportunistic eyes watched with delight as the fragile surface of stability crumbled, seizing the moment to strengthen support for insurgents in the south.

Yet, amidst the turmoil, a shade threatened on the horizon—a specter that would shape the course of history in ways unforeseen. Just three weeks after Diem's demise, tragedy struck once more as the echoes of gunfire rang out in Dallas, claiming the life of President Kennedy. In the wake of his assassination, Vice-President Lyndon B. Johnson ascended to the highest office in the land, vowing to uphold America's commitment to South Vietnam.

As the war machine churned into motion, the conflict in Vietnam took on new dimensions as the United States ramped up its military involvement and embarked on a path of "Americanization." Yet, another rhetoric of defense and containment, deeper currents flowed, framing the conflict within the broader context of the Cold War.

For the Saigon governments and their Western allies, the coup was portrayed as a necessary defense against the specter of armed violence and political upheaval. However, for the North Vietnamese and the National Liberation Front, the struggle was a noble quest to reunite a divided nation and repel the encroaching forces of foreign aggression—a battle cry that resonated with the sentiments of old, echoing the war against the French.

Chapter 4

Escalation and Americanization, 1963-1968

Gulf of Tonkin and the Westmoreland Expansion

On July 27, 1964, an enormous decision sent shockwaves through the halls of power, as 5,000 extra military advisers were dispatched to the embattled shores of South Vietnam, making the whole U.S. troop level 21,000. With their arrival, the stage was set for a dramatic escalation of America's involvement in the conflict, propelling the nation ever closer to the high ground of all-out war.

But destiny had other plans in store, as events unfolded that would forever alter the course of history. On the fateful evening of August 4, 1964, amidst the dark waters of the North Vietnamese coast, the destroyer USS Maddox found itself thrust into the ordeal of conflict. In a harrowing encounter, three torpedo boats of the North Vietnamese navy launched a brazen assault, plunging the region into chaos and uncertainty.

With the roar of gunfire echoing across the waves, the USS Maddox, aided by aircraft from the mighty USS Ticonderoga, bravely stood its ground, engaging the enemy with fierce determination. In the heat of battle, the tide turned in favor of the American forces as they inflicted heavy damage upon their opponents, sending a clear message of resolve to friend and foe alike.

However, in the chaos and confusion of war, the truth remained unreachable. Despite claims of a North Vietnamese attack, evidence later emerged suggesting that no such assault had taken place—a sobering revelation that cast doubt upon the events of that disastrous night.

While the dust settled on the waters of the Gulf of Tonkin, the stage was set for a new phase in

America's military involvement in Vietnam. Led by the indomitable General William Westmoreland, the United States embarked on a bold expansion of its military presence, determined to crush the forces of communism and secure victory at any cost.

But as the conflict twisted ever deeper into the abyss of war, questions lingered, haunting the collective conscience of a nation torn apart by division and strife. With each passing day, the toll of human suffering mounted, casting a shadow over the noble ideals that had once inspired America's intervention in Vietnam.

As reports of a supposed attack reached the hallowed halls of Washington, confusion reigned supreme, shrouding the truth in a veil of uncertainty. Yet, for the administration, the incident presented an opportunity—a device for the pursuit of greater military intervention.

Before the ink had dried on the reports, President Johnson seized upon the moment, appearing before the nation to announce retaliatory strikes against North Vietnamese targets. In a televised address that reverberated across the land, the die was cast, and the path to war laid bare.

Yet, even as the drums of conflict echoed across the horizon, the full extent of the truth remained shrouded in darkness. It would not be until the publication of the Pentagon Papers in 1969 that the American people would learn the full story—a tale of deception and manipulation that had led them down the path of war.

Fuelled by the administration's assertions of "unprovoked aggression," Congress rallied behind the cause, passing the Southeast Asia Resolution—better known as the Gulf of Tonkin Resolution. In a move that granted the president sweeping powers, Congress effectively handed him a blank check to wage war without the constraints of a formal declaration.

With unanimous approval in the House of Representatives and minimal opposition in the Senate, the resolution stood as a testament to the fervor of the times—a symbol of the nation's resolve to confront the specter of communism in the distant jungles of Vietnam.

Operation Rolling Thunder, 1965-1968

February 1965, the tranquil skies above Pleiku erupted in a storm of violence, as guerrilla forces launched a brazen assault on a U.S. air base, leaving death and destruction in their wake. The bloodshed of over a dozen U.S. personnel ignited a firestorm of retaliation, setting the stage for a conflict that would engulf the nation in turmoil.

With grim determination, the administration ordered retaliatory strikes against North Vietnam, unleashing Operation Flaming Dart—a precursor to the relentless onslaught that soon followed.

Enter Operation Rolling Thunder—a relentless barrage of bombs and missiles that rained down upon the beleaguered land of North Vietnam. Born of a desire to strengthen the morale of the South Vietnamese and signal rebellion to Hanoi, Rolling Thunder evolved into a relentless campaign of destruction aimed at breaking the will of the enemy and shattering their resolve.

With each passing day, the skies over North Vietnam became a battleground as U.S. aircraft unleashed their fury upon carefully selected targets. Yet, as the conflict dragged on, the goals of Rolling Thunder shifted, morphing into a crusade to cripple the very foundations of the North's industrial might and infrastructure.

For years, the skies reverberated with the thunderous roar of engines and the thunderous explosions of bombs, as more than a million attacks were flown and three-quarters of a million tons of ordnance rained down upon the land below.

But even as the campaign reached its zenith, the resolve of the North remained unbroken, their determination to resist undiminished. As the toll of death and destruction mounted, Rolling Thunder ground to a halt on November 11, 1968—a bitter testament to the futility of war.

Yet, even as one chapter closed, another opened—a new campaign, Operation Commando Hunt, sought to stem the flow of men and supplies along the notorious Hồ Chí Minh Trail, casting the nation deeper into the crucible of conflict.

The Big Build-Up

A new chapter in the history of Vietnam began to emerge amid the shifting tides of politics and power; this phase was characterized by the unstoppable ascent of American dominance and the convergence of coalition forces on the battlefield.

With a stroke of his pen, President Johnson set the stage for a dramatic escalation of American involvement, appointing General William C. Westmoreland to lead the charge as Commander of MACV. Under Westmoreland's stewardship, the American presence in Vietnam swelled from a mere 16,000 troops in 1964 to a staggering force of over 553,000 by 1969—a veritable tidal wave of firepower that swept across the land.

While the shade of conflict threatened, the ANZUS Pact allies, Australia and New Zealand, pledged their support, joining forces with the United States in a coalition of unprecedented scale. With their commitment, the ranks of the allied forces swelled, strengthened by the arrival of troops from the Republic of Korea, Thailand, and the Philippines—

each nation answering the call to arms in defense of freedom.

Yet, even as the military machine churned into motion, political affairs in Saigon reached a semblance of stability with the installation of the Thieu and Ky governments—a beacon of legitimacy in a sea of uncertainty.

But as the wheels of war turned, the need for logistical support became paramount. American airbases and facilities sprung up across the land, manned by brave souls tasked with defending them from enemy incursions. On March 8, 1965, the shores of Da Nang bore witness to the arrival of 3,500 United States Marines—the vanguard of American combat troops in South Vietnam.

In the days that followed, the conflict spilled onto the land, as the 173rd Airborne Brigade and other U.S. Army units joined the battle. On August 18, Operation Starlite heralded the dawn of a new era—a relentless ground assault that struck at the heart of the enemy's stronghold in Quảng Ngãi Province.

But as the smoke cleared and settled, the NLF Cong proved a resilient foe, adapting to the rigors of American-style warfare with cunning and guile.

In the waning months of 1964, the winds of war swept across the verdant landscapes of Vietnam, as the North Vietnamese shipped troops southward, heralding the dawn of a new phase in the conflict.

Within the corridors of power in Hanoi, debate raged over the best course of action, with some advocating for an immediate invasion of the south. A bold plan emerged—a daring scheme to divide southern Vietnam in two, using PAVN units to carve a path through the rugged terrain of the Central Highlands.

The stage sets as the opponents converge on the battlefield during Operation Silver Bayonet famously known as the Battle of the Ia Drang. Amidst the chaos and carnage of combat, both sides wrestled with the harsh realities of war, each learning valuable lessons in the burden of conflict.

For the North Vietnamese, the brutal engagement exacted a heavy toll, yet it also served as a trial of adaptation. Confronted with overwhelming

American superiority in air power and technology, they began to evolve, honing their tactics and strategies to confront their formidable foe.

Meanwhile, for the Americans, the battle shattered preconceived notions, dispelling the myth of the North Vietnamese as a mere band of guerrillas. Instead, they confronted a disciplined and highly motivated force—a formidable adversary that commanded respect and demanded attention.

Search and Destroy

In the hallowed halls of the Pentagon, a solemn declaration resounded—a call to arms that would forever alter the course of the conflict. On November 27, 1965, amidst the backdrop of escalating hostilities, the brass of the U.S. military declared a stark truth: to neutralize the North Vietnamese and NLF forces, to accomplish drastic escalation in troop levels was imperative.

With resolve hardened by the crucible of war, General Westmoreland, the architect of America's strategy, pressed his case before President Johnson in a series of meetings held in Honolulu in February 1966. His message was clear: the current U.S. presence had stemmed the tide of defeat but to achieve victory, more boots on the ground were needed.

Heeding the counsel of his military advisors, President Johnson authorized a monumental increase in troop strength, swelling the ranks to a staggering 429,000 by August 1966. With this influx of manpower, MACV embarked on a relentless campaign of operations, each more ambitious and audacious than the last.

For the brave men on the front lines, the war became a relentless odyssey of hardship and heroism. From the dense jungles of Vietnam to the scorching heat of the countryside, they marched tirelessly, their spirits tempered by the twin crucibles of boredom and terror.

Yet, amidst the chaos and confusion, it was the enemy who held sway over the ebb and flow of battle. The PAVN/NLF, with their guerrilla tactics and indomitable spirit, dictated the tempo of the conflict, striking with deadly precision before melting away into the shadows.

As the war raged on, Hanoi matched America's every move, funneling manpower and supplies along the infamous trails of Ho Chi Minh and Sihanouk. In the face of overwhelming odds, they stood resolute—a testament to the resilience of a nation determined to defend its independence.

In the swirling maelstrom of war, Vietnam became the arena for a clash of titans—a showdown between the indomitable elephant of American might and the elusive tiger of Vietnamese resolve. And amidst the chaos and carnage, the fate of a nation hung, as the forces of history converged on the blood-soaked fields of Vietnam.

The Ho Chi Minh Trail

In the complex corridors of war, North Vietnam forged a lifeline—a strategic artery that ticked with the flow of men and equipment, defying the relentless onslaught of American might. This lifeline bore the name bestowed upon it by the enemy—The Ho Chi Minh Trail, or as the North Vietnamese dubbed it, the Truong Son Strategic Supply Route.

From the bustling ports and rail hubs of the north, this vital artery snaked its way southward, carrying with it the lifeblood of the communist insurgency. Through rugged terrain and hostile landscapes, PAVN manpower and essential supplies embarked on an odyssey fraught with peril, their destination was the borderlands of South Vietnam.

But the Trail was more than a mere conduit of war—it was a testament to the ingenuity and determination of a nation under siege. Forging through the neutral territories of Laos and Cambodia, the Trail defied all attempts at interdiction, its tendrils reaching deep into the heart of enemy territory.

For the United States, the Trail presented a conundrum—a Gordian knot that defied easy solutions. To block the flow of men and supplies meant violating the sovereignty of neutral nations— a step too far, even in the crucible of war. Instead, a covert aerial interdiction campaign was launched in

Laos, a shadowy struggle that would persist until the bitter end.

However, Laos and Cambodia were not mere spectators in the conflict. In Laos, the Pathet Lao waged a fierce insurgency against the Royal Lao armed forces, supported by the clandestine efforts of the CIA-sponsored Hmong army and the thunderous bombs of the U.S. Air Force.

Prince Norodom Sihanouk moved a delicate political waltz, treading the fine line between East and West. In a bold plot, he struck a deal with the Chinese, allowing North Vietnamese forces to establish bases within his borders in exchange for payments and a share of the spoils of war.

The Tet Offensive

In the nightfall of 1967, General Westmoreland painted a notion of optimism—a vision where U.S. forces could soon be phased out of the war, their burdens transferred to the shoulders of the ARVN. Yet, as the New Year dawned, Vietnam stood poised on the brink of chaos.

On January 30, 1968, amidst the festivities of the Lunar New Year, the tranquility of the truce was shattered. With audacious ferocity, PAVN and NLF forces launched their most daring offensive yet—a relentless assault aimed at sparking a "General Uprising" among the South Vietnamese.

From bustling cities to fortified military installations, no corner of South Vietnam was spared as the enemy surged forth. The Americans and their South Vietnamese allies, caught off guard by the scale of the onslaught, rallied swiftly, dealing devastating blows to their foes.

Though the Communist forces suffered heavy losses, their resilience remained unbroken. But it was not the battlefield alone where victory was won or lost—far from it. In the realm of public perception, the Tet Offensive dealt a fatal blow to the political aspirations of Lyndon Johnson.

As the smoke settled on the blood-soaked fields of Vietnam, a wave of change swept across America. Senator Robert Kennedy emerged as a beacon of hope, announcing his bid for the Democratic nomination in the upcoming presidential election.

And then, in a moment that reverberated around the world, Johnson uttered words that would forever alter the course of history. "I shall not seek, and I will not accept, the nomination of my party for another term as your president," he declared, pledging his remaining time in office to the pursuit of peace in Vietnam.

Johnson declared that the United States would not only attack North Vietnam up to the boundary line and that American delegates were ready to meet with their North Vietnamese counterparts anywhere in the world "to discuss ways to bring this brutal war to an end." Much to Johnson's surprise, Hanoi agreed to communicate between the two sides a few days later. The Paris peace negotiations started on May 13.

Paris Peace Talks

The echoes of diplomacy resonated as nations wobbled on the rise of peace or prolonged conflict. On October 12, 1967, Secretary of State Dean Rusk's words rang out, a resolute declaration that echoed the frustrations of a nation entangled in the web of war. Yet, amidst the futility of peace initiatives, a ray of hope emerged—a hint of possibility that beckoned toward a path of reconciliation.

In the aftermath of the Tet Offensive, Lyndon Johnson found himself at a crossroads, grappling with the harsh realities of a conflict that defied resolution. His once steadfast resolve wavered, replaced by a newfound urgency to extricate his nation from the morass of war. The strategic gambits of Rolling Thunder had faltered, and the stalemate on the ground had yielded no decisive victories. Now, his singular focus turned toward the elusive prospect of peace.

Amidst the fog of war, U.S. and DRV negotiators converged on the hallowed grounds of Paris on May 10, 1968, for the inaugural session of peace talks. Across the table sat Xuan Thuy, the esteemed head of the DRV delegation, facing off against the seasoned diplomat Averell Harriman, the American ambassador-at-large.

Yet, for five interminable months, the halls of diplomacy echoed with discord, as entrenched positions and irreconcilable demands stymied progress. Hanoi, steadfast in its resolve, demanded an end to the bombing raids over North Vietnam, while Washington insisted on reciprocal measures to stem North Vietnamese military activities in the South. The delicate dance of diplomacy seemed poised on a knife's edge, as each side awaited the other's concession.

Adding to the complexity of the negotiations, delegations from the NLF and the South Vietnamese government awaited their turn at the bargaining table, further muddying the waters of diplomacy with competing agendas and divergent interests.

In the hushed chambers of diplomacy, the fate of nations hung in the balance—a delicate dance of power and persuasion unfolding against the backdrop of conflict. Neither side yielded, locked in a bitter stalemate that stretched into the waning days of October.

It was President Johnson who, in a bold stroke of diplomacy, issued preliminary orders to halt the relentless bombing raids over North Vietnam—a pivotal moment that thawed the icy grip of hostility and paved the way for peace talks to commence. As the dust settled, a glimmer of hope emerged on the horizon.

In the political arena, the stage raised for a dramatic showdown. Vice-President Hubert H. Humphrey, the standard-bearer of the Democratic Party, mounted a formidable challenge to his Republican rival, Richard M. Nixon. Riding the wave of momentum, Humphrey narrowed the gap, buoyed by his bold stance in calling for an end to the bombing campaign.

Yet, in the fervor of the electoral battle, Nixon harbored fears that victory would slip through his grasp. In a secrets maneuver, he reached out to South Vietnamese President Thieu, urging him to withhold his participation in the peace talks—a calculated plot aimed at securing an electoral edge.

And as the nation held its breath, the results of the election dangled. In a narrow victory, Nixon emerged triumphant, propelled to the presidency by the thinnest of margins. But as everything settled and the tumult of the campaign subsided, little had been achieved in the halls of diplomacy.

For all the glorious promises and political maneuvering, the Paris peace talks yielded little more than the shape of the negotiating table—a perfect reminder of the complexities and challenges that lay ahead on the road to peace.

Chapter 5

Vietnamization and American Withdrawal, 1969-1974

Richard Nixon's Pursuit of Peace with Honor

Throughout his campaign and into his presidency, Nixon championed a promise that resonated with a war-weary nation—he had a plan to bring an end to the Vietnam War. His vision was clear: to chart a course that would not only extricate American forces but also ensure the defense of South Vietnam.

Under the banner of the "Nixon Doctrine," the strategy of Vietnamization took root—an ambitious endeavor to empower the South Vietnamese armed forces, granting them the capacity to safeguard their nation with modern weaponry. It was a calculated gamble, a bid to shift the burden of defense onto the shoulders of the Vietnamese themselves.

But Nixon's ambitions extended beyond the borders of Vietnam. With an eye toward global diplomacy, he sought a historic breakthrough in relations with China and the Soviet Union—a feat that would reshape the geopolitical landscape. His overtures, rooted in realpolitik, ushered in an era of détente, marked by nuclear arms reductions and a thawing of tensions.

In Nixon's calculus, Vietnam was but one piece of a larger puzzle—a calculated move in the intricate dance of superpower relations. Yet, even as he navigated the complexities of international diplomacy, he remained steadfast in his commitment to South Vietnam, determined to forestall its inevitable collapse.

Teaming up with his trusted adviser, Henry Kissinger, Nixon employed a delicate balance of foreign policy gambits, leveraging Chinese and Soviet interests to quell domestic opposition to the war and secure progress at the negotiating table in Paris.

For a time, Nixon's strategy bore fruit. He succeeded in persuading the Soviets and the Chinese to curtail their military support for Vietnam, framing the move as a step toward broader strategic goals. But as the tumult of the Watergate scandal eroded his domestic support, the tide of Soviet assistance to Vietnam surged once more—a bitter reminder of the fragile balance of power in the pursuit of peace with honor.

Operation Menu and the Cambodian Incursion, 1969-1970

Prince Sihanouk of Cambodia found himself navigating dangerous political moistures as 1969 unfolded. Faced with mounting pressures from Cambodia's right-wing factions, he began to ride away from his once staunchly pro-left stance. In a bid for normalized relations with the United States, he forged an alliance with General Lon Nol, signaling a quaky shift in Cambodian politics.

Seizing on this change, President Nixon sanctioned a secret bombing campaign of unprecedented scale—an operation veiled in secrecy known as Operation Menu. For 14 relentless months, Cambodia's eastern border bore the brunt of B-52 strikes, raining down a staggering 2,756,941 tons of bombs. The devastation was unfathomable, eclipsing even the horrors of World War II.

Amidst the chaos, Sihanouk found himself ousted from power while on a diplomatic mission abroad. In a swift and decisive move, Lon Nol ascended to the Cambodian throne, slamming shut the ports to North Vietnamese military supply lines and demanding the expulsion of PAVN forces from the borderlands.

With the Cambodian government in flux, Nixon seized the opportunity to launch a military incursion, unleashing U.S. and South Vietnamese troops into Cambodian territory. Their mission: to dismantle PAVN/NLF sanctuaries and buy crucial time for the impending American withdrawal.

The incursion unearthed a trove of intelligence and logistical assets, disrupting enemy operations and yielding critical gains for the allied forces. Yet, it also unwittingly catalyzed a chain of events that would plunge Cambodia into further turmoil.

While PAVN forces retreated deeper into Cambodian territory, the country rocked on the brink of instability. The North Vietnamese, compelled to openly support their embattled allies, the Khmer Rouge, unwittingly fueled their rise to power.

In the aftermath of the incursion, South Vietnamese troops unleashed a wave of violence, tarnishing their reputation and emboldening support for the communist cause. Meanwhile, Sihanouk, exiled to China, lent his backing to the Khmer Rouge, the North Vietnamese, and the Pathet Lao, further entangling Cambodia in the web of Indochina's tumultuous politics.

The Easter Offensive

In the spring of 1972, Vietnamization faced its sternest trial as North Vietnamese forces unleashed a sweeping onslaught across the DMZ. With the onset of the Easter Offensive, later dubbed the Nguyen Hue Offensive by the North, the conflict surged to new heights.

Commencing on March 30, the offensive swiftly engulfed South Vietnam's northernmost provinces, including the pivotal Quang Tri City. Like a tide of steel, PAVN troops surged southward, their sights set on the historic city of Hue.

April brought further onslaughts from the North. From Cambodia's depths emerged a formidable three-division assault, supported by tanks and artillery, striking fear into the heart of An Loc in Binh Long Province. Simultaneously, another spearhead thrust from the tri-border region into the Central Highlands, seizing ARVN outposts and advancing menacingly toward Kontum, threatening to cleave South Vietnam in two.

In response, the U.S. mustered its aerial might, bolstering ARVN defenses and unleashing Operation Linebacker—the first bombardment of North Vietnam since the cessation of bombings in 1968. Despite the ferocity of the assaults on Hue, An Loc, and Kontum, the ARVN held firm, repelling the invaders and mounting a counteroffensive in May to reclaim lost ground.

By September 10, the proud flag of South Vietnam fluttered once more over the Citadel of Quang Tri City, marking a symbolic victory. Yet, the triumph was fleeting as the ARVN offensive faltered, ceding the reclaimed territory back to the North. The resilience displayed by South Vietnam came at a stark cost—underscoring its reliance on American air power for survival.

Meanwhile, the American exodus continued unabated, with troop numbers dwindling to less than 100,000 by the year's outset. By June, a mere six infantry battalions remained, and on August 12, the final contingent of American ground combat troops bid farewell to the war-torn land, leaving South Vietnam to confront its destiny alone.

U.S. Presidential Election of 1972 and Operation Linebacker II

As the political storm of the 1972 presidential election gathered momentum, the war once again took center stage. President Nixon's decision to halt Operation Linebacker on October 22, following a tentative agreement with North Vietnamese negotiators, set the stage for a dramatic turn of events. With the head of the U.S. negotiating team, Henry Kissinger, proclaiming "peace is at hand" just days before the election, Nixon's opponent, Senator McGovern, found his campaign further imperiled.

However, the path to peace proved treacherous. South Vietnamese President Thieu's staunch opposition to the agreement, particularly the provision allowing North Vietnamese troops to remain within South Vietnam, plunged negotiations into disarray. Thieu's insistence on demanding significant amendments derailed progress, prompting a standoff with the North.

To assert American resolve and reassure Thieu, Nixon unleashed Operation Linebacker II—a ferocious bombing campaign targeting Hanoi and Haiphong, commencing on December 18. Despite facing domestic and international outcry, Nixon remained resolute, attributing the impasse to North Vietnamese obstinacy.

Dubbed "War by tantrum" by critics, Nixon's heavy-handed approach garnered significant backlash. Yet, undeterred, he pressed on until December 29, intensifying pressure on Thieu to acquiesce to the revised terms of the agreement. As the political landscape trembled under the weight of war and negotiation, Nixon's actions cast a long shadow over both the election and the ongoing struggle for peace in Vietnam.

Return to Paris

On January 15, 1973, a pivotal moment emerged as President Nixon, citing advancements in peace talks, declared the cessation of all offensive actions against North Vietnam. This proclamation heralded a significant turn of events, signaling the imminent withdrawal of all U.S. troops from the embattled region. The stage was set for a historic milestone in the form of the Paris Peace Accords, formally titled "Ending the War and Restoring Peace in Vietnam," inked on January 27.

The accords, a culmination of arduous negotiations, delineated a roadmap for peace. Central to the agreement was the mandated withdrawal of all American personnel and the reciprocal release of prisoners of war. Within the borders of South Vietnam, a delicate ceasefire was to be enacted under the oversight of a multinational, 1,160-strong International Control Commission.

However, the accord's promise of tranquility belied the simmering tensions on the ground. Despite the ceasefire, both the Army of the Republic of Vietnam

(ARVN) and the People's Army of Vietnam/National Liberation Front (PAVN/NLF) vied for territorial dominance, escalating skirmishes and territorial disputes. The envisioned compromise political solution, including the possibility of a coalition government, remained elusive amidst the fractious landscape.

The signing of the accords marked a seminal moment, garnering global attention and acclaim. Notably, it prompted the prestigious Nobel Peace Prize to be conferred upon Henry Kissinger, the chief American negotiator, and Le Duc Tho, a prominent North Vietnamese counterpart.

In a rebellious twist of uncertainty, the passing of former President Lyndon Johnson just five days before the accord's signing highlighted the profound historical legacy of America's entanglement in the Vietnam War. served as a poignant reminder of the journey that had brought the world to this moment of tentative peace.

In the aftermath of the Vietnam War, a series of pivotal events unfolded, reshaping the line of diplomacy and conflict. The release of the first U.S.

prisoners of war by North Vietnam on February 11 marked a sad moment of transition. With all U.S. military personnel ordered to depart South Vietnam by March 29, the stage was set for a critical juncture in the pursuit of peace.

However, promises made by President Nixon to support South Vietnam's defense efforts faltered amidst the political tempest brewing on the home front. Caught in the throes of the Watergate Scandal and facing mounting opposition from a disillusioned Congress, Nixon found his ability to sway public opinion waning. Despite assurances of financial and limited military assistance, the reality of political turmoil hindered his capacity to fulfill commitments to President Thieu.

As Nixon's grip on power weakened, the fabric of international relations underwent a profound shift. Economic aid to South Vietnam dwindled, plagued by corruption within the government ranks, while North Vietnam's ties with the Soviet Union flourished, bolstering its military capabilities. With the United States gradually disengaging from the conflict, both superpowers reassessed their strategic priorities, diminishing the war's significance in their geopolitical calculus.

Within this growing landscape, North Vietnam seized the initiative, launching a formidable military offensive against the South. As the balance of power tilted decisively, the echoes of conflict reverberated anew, underscoring the complexities of peace and the enduring legacy of a nation divided.

Chapter 6

South Vietnam Stands Alone, 1974 – 1975

Total U.S. Withdrawal

Changes were on the air in Congress as the political climate in Washington changed. In December 1974, the Democratic majority wielded its power, passing the Foreign Assistance Act of 1974. This legislative strikeout cut all military funding to the South Vietnamese government and cast a shadow of uncertainty over the hard-won peace terms negotiated by Nixon. The uproar of Watergate had driven Nixon from office, leaving Gerald R. Ford to navigate the stormy swamps of presidential leadership.

Ford, stepping into the breach left by his predecessor, faced a daunting challenge. Despite his efforts to stem the tide, his veto of the Foreign Assistance Act was swiftly overridden by Congress, signaling a decisive break in America's commitment to its erstwhile ally.

By 1975, South Vietnam found itself standing on a precarious precipice, its fate staggering in the balance. With the withdrawal of American military support, the once-proud South Vietnamese Army stood alone against the relentless onslaught of the North Vietnamese forces. Chaos brewed within the borders of the embattled nation, a testament to the vacuum left by the departing Americans.

Economically crippled and politically adrift, South Vietnam wrestled with the aftershocks of its shattered alliance. The departure of U.S. troops had dealt a wrecking blow to an economy propped up by American generosity. Moreover, the global impact of the Arab oil embargo and subsequent economic downturn sent shockwaves through the fragile economic fabric of the nation.

Between the signing of the Paris Accord and the waning months of 1974, a fragile peace hovered over Vietnam, highlighted by sporadic brawls over contested territories. Yet, beneath the veneer of calm, tensions steamed, fueled by the impatience of the North Vietnamese leadership with the obstinacy of the Thieu regime in Saigon.

As whispers of discontent swirled within Hanoi's circles of power, a pivotal decision emerged from the Politburo: a limited offensive into Phuoc Long Province, emerging from the sanctuary of Cambodia's borders. This strategic move aimed to test Saigon's resolve, gauge American reaction, and address logistical concerns on the ground.

With swift precision, the Vietnamese People's Army (VPA) swept through Phuoc Long, seizing control without invoking the wrath of American air power. The absence of U.S. intervention emboldened Hanoi, propelling them to reassess their strategic calculus. General Van Tien Dung, entrusted with the mantle of command, received a solemn charge from First Party Secretary Le Duan, underscoring the gravity of the moment.

While General Van set his sights on Pleiku in the Central Highlands, the echoes of Le Duan's words resonated through the corridors of power in Hanoi. "Never have we held military and political conditions so excellent or a strategic benefit so awesome as we have now."

Campaign 275

On March 10, 1975, the opening salvo of General Dung's master plan reverberated through the Central Highlands as Campaign 275 surged into action. With tanks rumbling and heavy artillery thundering, the Vietnamese People's Army (VPA) set its sights on Ban Me Thuot, nestled in Darlac

Province. Victory here would not only secure the town but also pave the way for a strategic thrust toward Pleiku and the coastal route, setting the stage for future offensives.

The Army of the Republic of Vietnam (ARVN), ill-prepared and outmatched, crumbled before the relentless onslaught, capitulating on March 11. The swift collapse of ARVN defenses caught Hanoi off guard, propelling General Van to urge the Politburo for an immediate advance on Pleiku and Kontum, seizing the opportunity presented by favorable weather conditions.

Meanwhile, in Saigon, President Thieu grappled with mounting apprehension, fearing the encirclement of his forces in the northern provinces and Central Highlands. His decision to redeploy troops southward, under the guise of a "lighten the top and keep the bottom" strategy, quickly descended into chaos as the VPA launched a surprise attack from the north.

Caught in a maelstrom of violence and desperation, ARVN forces attempted a precarious retreat, with General Phu leading a harrowing exodus toward the coast. Pleiku and Kontum fell, abandoned in the face of overwhelming enemy advance, as the beleaguered ARVN forces, interspersed with civilian refugees, struggled against relentless shelling and enemy encroachment.

By April 1, the "column of tears," as it came to be known, dissolved into history, swallowed by the tumult of war and the relentless march of the Vietnamese People's Army. In the shadow of escalating conflict, the fate of Vietnam hung in the balance, poised on the precipice of a tumultuous chapter yet to unfold.

March 20 marked a climactic moment as President Thieu, amid mounting pressure, reversed course, issuing a desperate decree to hold Hue, the vibrant heart of Vietnam's cultural heritage, at any cost. Yet, as the North Vietnamese onslaught spread, chaos gripped the city, and the once-sturdy resolve of the Army of the Republic of Vietnam (ARVN) crumbled under the weight of relentless assault.

With eerie precision, the Vietnamese People's Army (VPA) encircled Hue, tightening their grip with each passing hour. As the siege tightened, a frantic exodus unfolded, with civilians flocking to the airport and docks, seeking refuge amidst the tempest of conflict. Some braved the treacherous waters, swimming to boats in a bid for salvation.

In the turmoil, the once-proud ARVN found themselves overwhelmed, their lines shattered in the face of overwhelming odds. In a grim tableau of despair, some South Vietnamese soldiers, consumed by panic, resorted to unthinkable acts, firing upon civilians in a desperate bid to secure passage for their own retreat.

On March 31, after a valiant but futile stand, Hue succumbed to the relentless onslaught, a city once vibrant now rendered a ghostly testament to the brutality of war. As the echoes of battle faded, Da Nang, its once bustling streets now eerily silent, faced the wrath of incoming rockets, heralding its inevitable fall.

By March 28, the relentless advance of the VPA loomed large on the outskirts, while the 30th witnessed a staggering capitulation, with over 100,000 ARVN troops laying down their arms, their morale shattered amidst the specter of defeat. With

Da Nang's fall, the last bastions of resistance crumbled, casting a shadow of despair over the Central Highlands and northern provinces.

Final North Vietnamese Offensive

With the northern reaches of Vietnam firmly under their control, the Politburo orchestrated a decisive move, tasking General Van with orchestrating a final offensive against Saigon. The audacious plan, codenamed the Ho Chi Minh Campaign, aimed to seize the capital before the onset of the monsoon, thwarting any chance of ARVN reconstitution.

Bolstered by recent triumphs, northern forces surged forward, claiming strategic cities with relentless efficiency. Nha Trang, Cam Ranh, and Da Lat fell like dominoes, paving the way for a climactic showdown on the doorstep of Saigon.

On April 7, the battle-scarred landscape witnessed a clash of titans as three North Vietnamese divisions descended upon Xuan-loc, a mere 40 miles east of Saigon. The ARVN 18th Infantry Division, facing overwhelming odds, mounted a valiant defense, engaging in a brutal struggle that would echo through the annals of history.

For two agonizing weeks, the fate of South Vietnam hung in the balance as the defenders, their resolve tested to its limits, fought tooth and nail to stave off the impending tide of conquest. Yet, by April 21, the inevitable became reality as the beleaguered garrison capitulated, casting a pall of despair over the embattled nation.

Amidst tears and bitterness, President Thiệu, a symbol of a vanquished era, relinquished power on April 21, denouncing the perceived betrayal by erstwhile allies. Departing for Taiwan, he left behind a nation teetering on the brink, its fate now entrusted to General Duong Van Minh.

As April drew to a close, the relentless advance of the North Vietnamese forces cast a shadow of inevitability over Saigon. Encircling the city with formidable strength, 100,000 troops hemmed in the beleaguered defenders, leaving them outnumbered and outgunned.

On April 29, as the clamor of conflict echoed through the streets, Operation Frequent Wind heralded the final chapter of the conflict. In a dramatic display of resolve, the largest helicopter evacuation in history happened, offering a fleeting glimpse of hope in the chaos and uncertainty that engulfed the city.

Fall of Saigon

In the waning days of April, a frenzied atmosphere gripped Saigon as chaos and desperation reigned supreme. casting a shadow of uncertainty over the city. In a hysterical bid to escape impending doom, South Vietnamese officials and civilians alike scrambled for safety, their hopes dashed against the backdrop of encroaching despair.

American helicopters, harbingers of salvation, embarked on a daring mission to evacuate both U.S. personnel and desperate South Vietnamese citizens from the besieged U.S. embassy. Delayed until the eleventh hour by Ambassador Graham Martin's unwavering belief in the city's resilience, the evacuations happened in scenes of pandemonium, with throngs of panicked Vietnamese clamoring for a chance at salvation.

In a pathetic plea for aid, Martin implored the U.S. government to extend a lifeline of $700 million to support South Vietnam's faltering defenses, but his appeals fell on deaf ears. Across the Pacific, the death knell tolled for South Vietnam, as President Ford's televised proclamation on April 23 marked the end of American support for the beleaguered regime.

Amidst the clamor of evacuation efforts, North Vietnamese tanks breached the city's defenses, inching ever closer to its heart. With each passing moment, the grip of inevitability tightened around Saigon's neck.

While dawn broke on April 30, the final chapter of Saigon's saga spread to a height of chaos. Against a backdrop of escalating violence, the last vestiges of American presence were whisked away by helicopter, leaving behind a city staggering on the brink.

With unrelenting force, VPA troops swept through the city, overwhelming all resistance in their path.

Vital installations fell like pieces, as the presidential palace succumbed to the triumphant wave of the NLF flag.

In a tragic moment of surrender, President Dương Văn Minh, Thieu's successor, sought to capitulate, only to be met with a sobering reality. Colonel Búi Tín, the voice of the victorious North Vietnamese forces, delivered a stark message: there was nothing left to surrender. With a heavy heart, Minh issued his final decree, ordering South Vietnamese troops to lay down their arms, as the curtain fell on Saigon's final stand.

Chapter 7

Aftermath

The fragile peace in Southeast Asia was shadowed by the strains of battle that continued long after the smoke had cleared from the burning remains of Saigon.

On May 15, 1975, a tragic end to America's rugged involvement evolved in the form of the Mayagüez incident, a daring rescue mission turned tragedy. Eighteen Marines and airmen met their fate in a scuffle with the Khmer Rouge on a remote island off the Cambodian coast, their names etched forever on the final panel of the Vietnam Veterans Memorial.

Meanwhile, the winds of change swept through Cambodia as the Khmer Rouge seized power, their ascent culminating in the capture of Phnom Penh on April 12. In a dramatic evacuation reminiscent of Saigon's fall, Operation Eagle Pull whisked away

U.S. Ambassador John G. Dean mere hours before the communist victors arrived.

With the Khmer Rouge's triumph, Cambodia plunged into darkness, its urban centers deserted as inhabitants were forcibly relocated to the countryside. Amidst the chaos, the vision of a Maoist utopia took shape in Democratic Kampuchea, heralding a new era filled with uncertainty and disruption.

On July 2, 1976, a watershed moment marked the consolidation of Vietnam's fate as both North and South were amalgamated into the Socialist Republic of Vietnam. Saigon, the once-vibrant capital of the South, bowed to the winds of change, reborn as Ho Chi Minh City in homage to the revered leader of the North.

Yet, the birth of a unified Vietnam was stained by the specter of retribution. Hundreds of thousands found themselves ensnared in the dragnet of reeducation camps, condemned as collaborators and traitors by the new regime, a grim testament to the price of allegiance to the fallen South Vietnamese government.

Meanwhile, North Vietnam wasted little time in extending its influence, exerting control over Laos, effectively reducing it to a puppet state. Yet, the specter of conflict loomed large as the Khmer Rouge, driven by territorial ambitions, kindled tensions along Vietnam's border.

The simmering animosities erupted into open warfare as Vietnamese forces launched a decisive invasion, toppling Pol Pot's genocidal regime and installing a pro-Vietnamese government. The Third Indochina War bore witness to Vietnam's turbulent quest for regional hegemony.

However, international recognition remained elusive as the U.S. and the United Nations persisted in viewing the Khmer Rouge, perpetrators of unspeakable atrocities, as allies. In a twist of fate, China, seething with indignation over Vietnam's audacity in vanquishing their Khmer Rouge brethren, launched a retaliatory invasion in 1979.

The conflict, characterized by ferocious battles and strategic stalemates, eventually petered out as both sides grappled with the grim realities of protracted warfare. In the end, the Chinese forces withdrew, leaving behind a scarred landscape and a region haunted by the specter of conflict.

Chapter 8

Other Countries' Involvement

The Soviet Union

Throughout the Vietnam War, the Soviet Union emerged as a steadfast ally of North Vietnam, providing crucial support that bolstered the communist cause. Arms, ammunition, and military equipment flowed incessantly from Soviet warehouses to the battlefields of Vietnam, sustaining the North Vietnamese war machine. Tanks rumbled across the landscape, planes soared through the skies, and helicopters whirred tirelessly, all bearing the imprint of Soviet craftsmanship.

Medical supplies poured in, healing the wounded and tending to the sick. The Soviet Union's contribution was not merely material; it extended to the realm of expertise as well. Hundreds of military advisers descended upon Vietnam, imparting their knowledge and honing the skills of the Vietnamese army. Among them, Soviet pilots stood out, serving not only as instructors but also as combatants, bravely taking to the skies in defense of the communist cause.

Despite the intensity of the conflict, the Soviet Union's casualties remained remarkably low. Less than a dozen of its citizens perished in the cauldron of war, a testament to the efficiency and caution with which Soviet support was extended. Yet, their impact on the course of the conflict was profound, shaping the course of the war and leaving a mark on the records of history.

People's Republic of China

The People's Republic of China, under the leadership of Chairman Mao Zedong, played a significant role in the Vietnam War, extending critical support to its communist ally, North Vietnam. The seeds of Chinese involvement were sown in the summer of 1962 when Mao Zedong made a pivotal decision to supply Hanoi with a formidable arsenal of 90,000 rifles and guns, a gesture of solidarity that came at no cost to the Vietnamese.

As Operation Rolling Thunder unleashed American firepower upon North Vietnam, China mobilized its resources to aid its beleaguered ally. Engineering battalions, accompanied by anti-aircraft units, were dispatched to the war-torn landscapes of North Vietnam. Their mission: was to repair the ravages of American bombing campaigns, reconstruct vital infrastructure including roads and railways, and undertake a myriad of engineering tasks. By shouldering this burden, Chinese support alleviated the pressure on North Vietnamese forces, enabling them to redirect their efforts toward the conflict raging in the South.

From 1965 to 1970, a staggering contingent of over 320,000 Chinese soldiers trod upon Vietnamese soil, marking a period of intense collaboration between the two communist nations. The zenith of this military alliance came in 1967, with a staggering 170,000 Chinese troops stationed in North Vietnam, bolstering its defenses and fortifying its resolve against the onslaught of American aggression.

Decades later, in April 2006, Vietnam paid tribute to the sacrifice of nearly 1,100 Chinese soldiers who laid down their lives in the crucible of war. An additional 4,200 Chinese soldiers bore the scars of conflict, their bodies testament to the enduring bonds forged in the crucible of battle. Through their unwavering support, the People's Republic of China left an indelible mark on the tumultuous tapestry of the Vietnam War, a testament to the enduring spirit of solidarity between nations united in the pursuit of a common cause.

Republic of Korea

South Korea, a staunch ally of the United States, played a pivotal role in the Vietnam War, with its military emerging as the second-largest foreign contingent deployed in South Vietnam. The involvement of South Korean troops in Vietnam unfolded gradually, with the first deployments commencing in 1964 and swelling in subsequent years.

The commitment of South Korea to the conflict became increasingly pronounced as large combat battalions began arriving on Vietnamese soil in 1965. Throughout the war, approximately 300,000 South Korean soldiers would be dispatched to Vietnam, forming a formidable force alongside their American counterparts. Like their U.S. allies, South Korean soldiers adhered to a rotation system, serving one-year tours before being replaced by fresh recruits. This relentless cycle persisted from 1964 until the withdrawal of South Korean troops in 1973.

At its peak, the South Korean military presence in Vietnam reached a formidable strength of 50,000 troops, a testament to Seoul's unwavering commitment to the conflict. However, this commitment exacted a heavy toll, with more than 5,000 South Korean soldiers laying down their lives on the battlefields of Vietnam, and an additional 11,000 sustaining injuries in the crucible of war.

The sacrifice of South Korean forces in Vietnam underscored the nation's steadfast dedication to the cause of freedom and democracy, cementing its place in the annals of history as a stalwart defender of liberty in the face of adversity.

Democratic People's Republic of Korea

In a decisive move orchestrated by the Korean Workers' Party in October 1966, the Democratic People's Republic of Korea (DPRK), commonly known as North Korea, embarked on a strategic intervention in the Vietnam War. Early in 1967, North Korea dispatched a formidable fighter squadron to North Vietnam, extending crucial support to the embattled North Vietnamese forces.

Tasked with bolstering the defenses of Hanoi, the North Korean fighter squadron seamlessly integrated with the North Vietnamese 921st and 923rd fighter squadrons, forming a formidable aerial alliance against the common adversary. The North Korean pilots exhibited unwavering resolve and skill as they navigated the treacherous skies over Vietnam, lending crucial air support to their Vietnamese counterparts.

Reports indicate that over 200 pilots from North Korea's elite ranks served in the conflict, demonstrating a steadfast commitment to the cause of their Vietnamese comrades. In a display of solidarity, North Korea also dispatched at least two anti-aircraft artillery regiments, further fortifying the defense capabilities of the North Vietnamese forces.

Beyond the deployment of personnel, North Korea's support extended to the provision of vital military supplies, including weapons, ammunition, and an impressive two million sets of uniforms. This comprehensive assistance underscored North Korea's unwavering dedication to the Vietnamese cause.

Echoing the sentiments of solidarity, North Korean leader Kim Il Sung delivered a resolute message to his pilots, urging them to "fight in the war as if the Vietnamese sky were their own." This rallying cry encapsulated the spirit of camaraderie and shared struggle that defined the collaboration between North Korea and North Vietnam during this pivotal chapter in history.

Australia and New Zealand

As staunch allies under the ANZUS Treaty, Australia and New Zealand played significant roles in the Vietnam War, driven by their shared commitment to counter the spread of communism in Southeast Asia. Drawing upon their experience in counterinsurgency tactics gleaned from the Malayan Emergency, both nations recognized the strategic importance of stemming communist expansion in the region.

Australia, in particular, demonstrated a robust commitment to the conflict, deploying a peak of 7,672 combat troops to Vietnam. In a bold move to bolster its military presence, Australia reintroduced conscription despite facing considerable public opposition to the war. New Zealand, while on a smaller scale, also made substantial contributions, sending 552 troops to join the fight alongside their Australian allies.

Most of these troops served under the banner of the 1st Australian Task Force, stationed in Phuoc Tuy Province, a testament to the close collaboration between the two nations in the theater of operations. Both countries initially dispatched advisers to Vietnam, gradually escalating their involvement until combat troops were fully committed by 1965.

New Zealand's contributions included diverse military assets, ranging from engineers and artillery batteries to special forces and regular infantry units. This multifaceted approach underscored New Zealand's commitment to providing comprehensive support to the Allied efforts in South Vietnam.

Throughout their deployments, Australian and New Zealand units showcased exemplary courage and determination, earning them prestigious U.S. unit citations in recognition of their valiant service. Their unwavering dedication to the cause exemplified the enduring spirit of camaraderie and cooperation that defined the alliance between Australia, New Zealand, and the United States during one of the most challenging chapters in modern history.

Thailand

From 1965 to 1971, Thai Army units, notably the renowned "Queen's Cobra" battalion, played a significant role in the Vietnam War, underscoring Thailand's commitment to the conflict. While Thai forces saw action in South Vietnam, their involvement extended further into the covert theater of Laos, where they engaged in a clandestine war from 1964 to 1972.

In Laos, Thai regular formations operated alongside the CIA-sponsored Police Aerial Reconnaissance Units (PARU), composed of skilled volunteers. These PARU operatives, though irregular, executed vital reconnaissance missions along the western stretches of the Ho Chi Minh Trail. Despite being outnumbered, their actions proved instrumental in gathering intelligence and disrupting enemy supply lines.

The covert operations conducted by Thai forces and PARU volunteers in Laos remain shrouded in mystery, often overshadowed by more prominent narratives of the Vietnam War. Yet, their contributions constitute a crucial chapter in the

Southeast Asian conflict, highlighting Thailand's vital role in regional security and its unwavering dedication to countering communist expansionism during a tumultuous period in history.

Canada

In the records of the Vietnam War, Canada's role emerges as a lesser-known but significant facet of the conflict. While Canada did not officially deploy troops to Vietnam, its citizens made a substantial contribution to the war effort, albeit through a different avenue.

Most notably, a considerable number of Canadians, estimated between 2,500 to 3,000, enlisted in the United States military and served in various capacities during the Vietnam War. These individuals, driven by a myriad of motivations, found themselves on the front lines of one of history's most contentious conflicts.

For many Canadians who donned the uniform of the U.S. military, their service in Vietnam marked a transformative period in their lives. Upon returning from the war, a significant portion of these individuals chose to become naturalized citizens of the United States. Others were already dual citizens before enlisting, reflecting the complex and interconnected nature of Canadian-American relations during this tumultuous era.

While Canada's direct involvement in the Vietnam War may have been limited, the contributions of its citizens who served in the conflict underscore the interconnectedness of nations and the shared sacrifices made in pursuit of common goals, even in the midst of distant conflicts across the globe.

Chapter 9

Use of Chemical Defoliants

The use of chemical defoliants stands as a controversial and haunting chapter, marked by its devastating impact on both the environment and human health, these tactics remain contentious and enduring as the widespread use of herbicides by the United States military. These chemical agents were deployed with the intent to strip away vegetation cover from vast swathes of land but left a lasting legacy of environmental destruction and human suffering in the regions where they were employed.

While the conflict escalated, American military strategists grappled with the challenge posed by dense jungle terrain, which provided ideal cover for enemy forces. In response, Operation Ranch Hand was initiated, a program aimed at defoliating areas surrounding both large and small base camps across Southeast Asia. Spearheaded by corporations such as Dow and Monsanto, the endeavor saw the development and deployment of a range of herbicides, each marked with distinctive color-coded bands.

Among the most notorious of these chemical agents was Agent Orange, infamous for its dioxin contamination. Throughout the American commitment to the war, approximately 12 million gallons of Agent Orange alone were sprayed across the region, leaving a toxic legacy that endures to this day. The Mekong Delta, a prime area of Operation Ranch Hand operations, bore witness to extensive defoliation efforts, particularly along its waterways where U.S. Navy patrol boats patrolled vulnerable to ambush from concealed enemy positions.

Decades after the cessation of hostilities, the aftermath of these chemical defoliation campaigns continues to unfold, with persistent environmental contamination, widespread disease, and intergenerational health impacts plaguing the affected regions. The legacy of Operation Ranch

Hand serves as a reminder of the far-reaching consequences of warfare, both for the land and its inhabitants.

In 1961-1962, under the authorization of the Kennedy administration, the United States commenced a campaign utilizing chemical weapons to destroy rice crops in Vietnam. Over six years, from 1961 to 1967, the U.S. Air Force indiscriminately sprayed approximately 20 million U.S. gallons of concentrated herbicides across vast swathes of land, encompassing an estimated 6 million acres. This aerial assault affected an alarming 13 percent of South Vietnam's territory, decimating crops and trees alike.

The consequences of this chemical onslaught were dire and enduring. A harrowing report published by the Wall Street Journal in 1997 revealed the staggering toll of dioxin-related deformities, with up to half a million children born with debilitating birth defects. Southern Vietnam bore the brunt of this tragedy, witnessing birth defect rates four times higher than those in the north.

Despite mounting evidence of its catastrophic effects, the use of chemical defoliants may have violated international rules of war at the time. A 1967 study conducted by the Agronomy Section of the Japanese Science Council painted a grim picture, attributing the destruction of 3.8 million acres of foliage to these toxic chemicals. Tragically, the collateral damage extended beyond vegetation, claiming the lives of countless peasants and livestock.

Decades later, the legacy of Agent Orange persists, haunting the Vietnamese population with the specter of dioxin poisoning. The Vietnamese government estimates that over 4,000,000 individuals have fallen victim to this silent scourge, with dioxin levels in some areas of southern Vietnam surpassing international safety standards by over 100 times.

The repercussions of Agent Orange also reverberate within the United States, where veterans exposed to the herbicides grapple with a myriad of health issues. The U.S. Veterans Administration has identified a range of conditions, including various cancers, diabetes, and birth defects in the offspring of exposed veterans, as potential side effects of Agent Orange exposure.

While debates persist regarding the legality and morality of using chemical defoliants in warfare, the enduring suffering wrought by these toxic substances serves as a solemn reminder of the profound human cost of armed conflict.

Conclusion

The lasting effects of a war that forever changed the path of history confront us as we draw to an end in our quest for knowledge of the chaotic terrain of the Vietnam War. From the rice paddies of South Vietnam to the halls of power in Washington, D.C., the Vietnam War was an ordeal of courage, sacrifice, and tragedy.

Throughout these pages, we have borne witness to the harrowing experiences of soldiers, diplomats, and civilians caught in the crossfire of war. We have seen the indomitable spirit of the human soul, as brave men and women from across the globe answered the call of duty, risking life and limb in the pursuit of freedom and justice.

Yet, amidst the chaos and devastation, there is also resilience and hope. For every tale of hardship, there is a story of triumph over adversity. For every loss, there is a lesson learned and a resolve strengthened. The Vietnam War, with all its complexities and contradictions, serves as a testament to the enduring power of the human spirit to persevere in the face of adversity.

While we bid farewell to these pages, let us not forget the lessons of the past. Let us honor the sacrifices of those who came before us by striving for a future marked by peace, understanding, and compassion. Let us remember that the true legacy of the Vietnam War lies not in the conflicts of the past, but in the possibilities of the future.

If you have found this journey through the Vietnam War to be enlightening and thought-provoking, I invite you to explore our other books, available on Amazon. From riveting historical accounts to inspiring biographies, there is a wealth of knowledge waiting to be discovered. Simply visit our Amazon author central page under "Charles William" to explore our collection.

By clicking the +Follow button on our author central page, you can stay updated on our latest releases and join a community of readers passionate about history and storytelling. Together, let us continue to explore the rich tapestry of human experience and draw inspiration from the stories that shape our world.

Thank you for joining me on this journey through the Vietnam War. May we carry the lessons of the past with us as we forge ahead into the future, guided by the timeless values of courage, resilience, and hope.

Printed in Great Britain
by Amazon